© SUSAETA EDICIONES, S.A. - Obra colectiva
Campezo, s/n - 28022 Madrid
Tel.: 913 009 100 - Fax: 913 009 118
ediciones@susaeta.com

This edition first published 2013 by
Brown Watson
The Old Mill, 76 Fleckney Road
Kibworth Beauchamp
Leicestershire LE8 0HG

ISBN: 978-0-7097-2150-5

© 2013 Brown Watson, English edition
Reprinted 2014, 2015, 2018

Printed in Malaysia

Encyclopedia
of
Dinosaurs

Brown Watson
ENGLAND

Contents

Animals before and during the time of dinosaurs 14

Prehistoric periods	CARBONIFEROUS
	PERMIAN
	TRIASSIC
	JURASSIC
	CRETACEOUS

Pterosaurs 30

Dinosaurs 36

Scientific Explanations 110

Dinosaur index 124

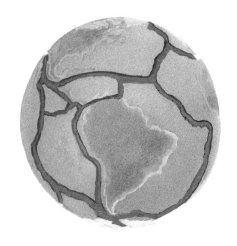

On the move

The Earth's crust has been on the move for millions of years. Some continents are gradually separating, and the plates collide to form mountain ranges. The Earth's surface looks very different now from the way it looked when the first dinosaurs were alive.

When plates slide, they create friction along the fault line and this can cause an earthquake.

The Earth's crust is made up of tectonic, oceanic and continental plates. These plates move a few centimetres each year.

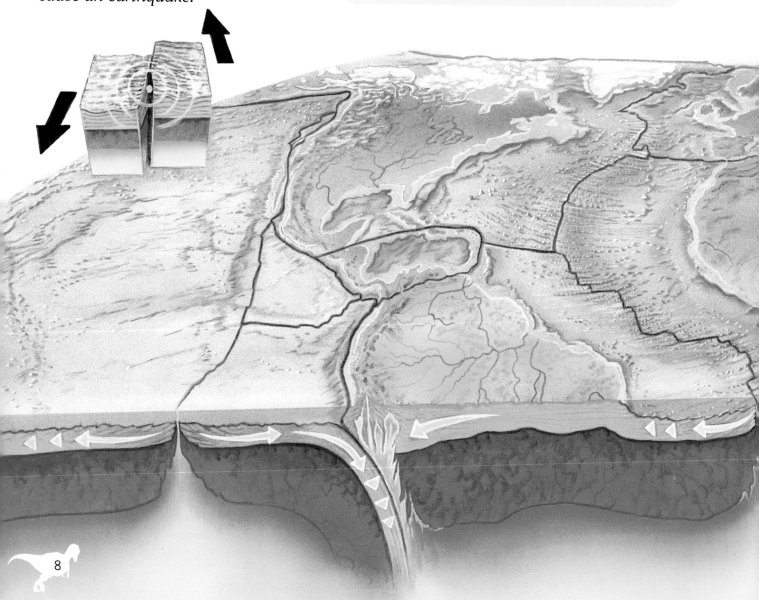

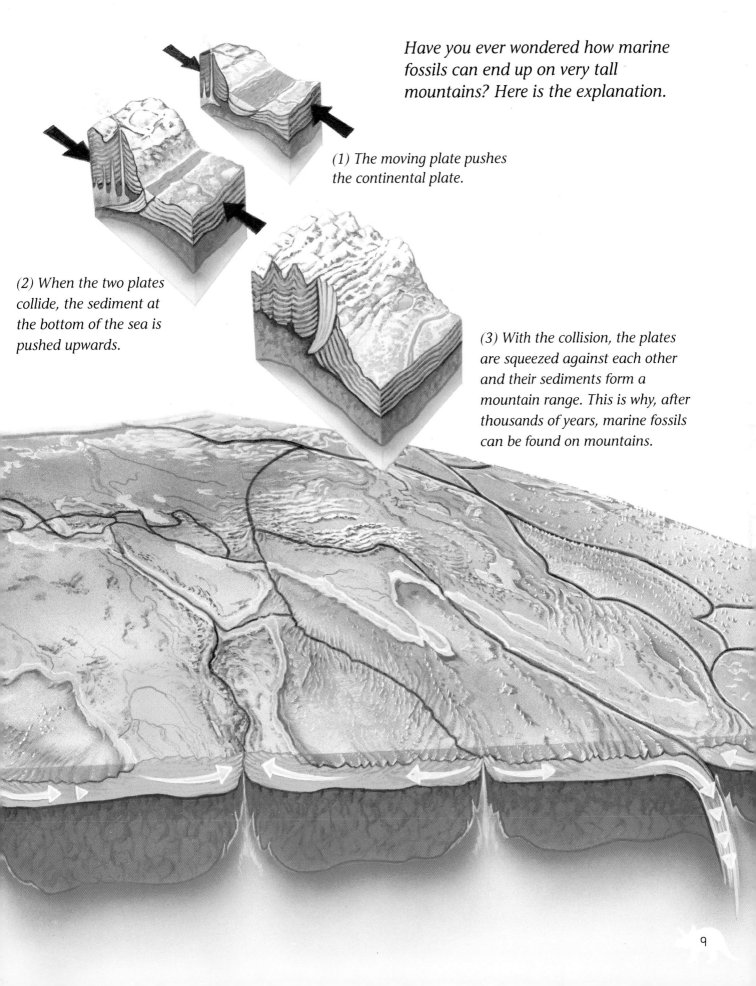

Have you ever wondered how marine fossils can end up on very tall mountains? Here is the explanation.

(1) The moving plate pushes the continental plate.

(2) When the two plates collide, the sediment at the bottom of the sea is pushed upwards.

(3) With the collision, the plates are squeezed against each other and their sediments form a mountain range. This is why, after thousands of years, marine fossils can be found on mountains.

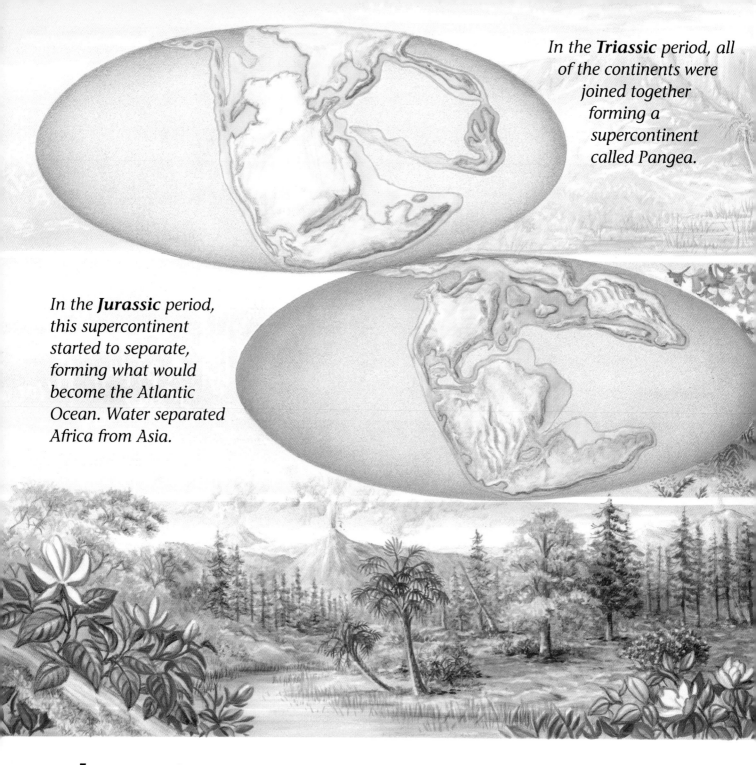

In the **Triassic** period, all of the continents were joined together forming a supercontinent called Pangea.

In the **Jurassic** period, this supercontinent started to separate, forming what would become the Atlantic Ocean. Water separated Africa from Asia.

Changing continents

The planet Earth – as well as its inhabitants – has changed significantly. These maps show how the continents have transformed over the course of millions of years, during the geologic periods of dinosaurs.

At the beginning of the Cretaceous period, the continents separated even more and the Earth started to divide into more fragments.

At the end of the Cretaceous period, South America and Africa were moving away from North America and Europe. The continents began to look like they do today.

11

The history of the Earth

To get an idea of life on our planet, the 5,000 million years of its existence have been condensed into a 12-hour clock. **Homo sapiens** (that's us!) have only been around for the final second of these 12 hours.

Only 90 minutes have passed since the first life forms appeared at the beginning of the Cambrian period. Dinosaurs lived from the Triassic to Cretaceous periods.

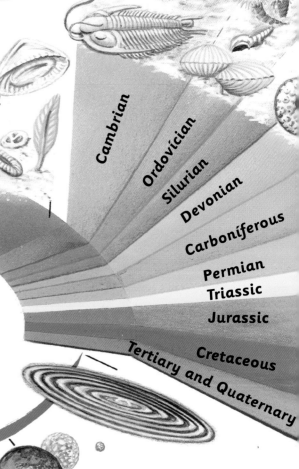

Cambrian

Ordovician

Silurian

Devonian

Carboniferous

Permian

Triassic

Jurassic

Cretaceous

Tertiary and Quaternary

Proterozoic Period

Archaic Period

*The whole period before life appeared on Earth, called the **Precambrian**, which includes the Archaic and Proterozoic periods, takes up more than 10 of the 12 hours.*

Humans have only existed for one second on this clock!

ANIMALS BEFORE
and **DURING** the
TIME of **DINOSAURS**

Hylonomus
The earliest reptile

This lizard-like creature belongs to the most primitive group of reptiles known, along with turtles and tortoises. Hylonomus fossils have been found in petrified tree trunks.

It is believed that, millions of years ago, the Hylonomus would go in search of insects and become trapped in hollow trunks.

Hylonomus The lack of opening in its skull shows that it is the most primitive reptile. This is also characteristic of the skulls of turtles and tortoises, which are the only survivors of this group. It ate insects and other invertebrates. Its shape and size were probably very similar to the modern lizard.

Small like lizards

HYLONOMUS: Its name is linked to wood, because it was discovered in tree trunks.
- **Discovery**: Nova Scotia, Canada
- **Size:** 20cm
- **Period:** late Carboniferous

17

Dimetrodon and Edaphosaurus

Reptiles with sails

These two creatures are sometimes called Pelycosaurs and were the transition between reptiles and mammals. They had a huge 'sail' on their back and scales on their belly, like a crocodile.

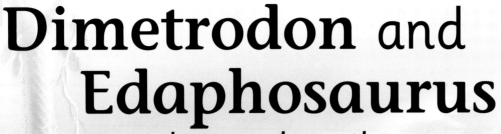

Big teeth

EDAPHOSAURUS means 'pavement lizard', named for its large, flat teeth.
- **Discovery:** Europe and North America
- **Size:** 3m long and 1.5m tall
- **Period:** early Permian

Dimetrodon A *carnivorous* reptile with large, sharp teeth. Its *sail* may have worked like a solar panel, keeping its blood *warm*. If, however its body temperature was too high, the sail would release heat and cool it down. It may also have been used for mating displays or to scare off predators.

Early meat eater
DIMETRODON means 'two shapes of teeth'.
• **Discovery:** Texas and Oklahoma, USA
• **Size:** 3m
• **Period:** early Permian

Edaphosaurus Looked very similar to the Dimetrodon, but it was a gentler animal, because it was a *herbivore* and had shorter teeth. Neither of them were dinosaurs but were part of the group Synapsida which includes all living mammals.

We can find out if an animal was a carnivore or a herbivore from the shape and size of its teeth.

19

Icarosaurus and Longisquama
Gliding reptiles

Some of the most primitive small reptiles could have been the earliest vertebrates to be able to glide through the air.

Greek myth

ICAROSAURUS means 'Icarus lizard' in reference to the Greek myth about the man who wished he could fly.
- **Discovery:** New Jersey, USA
- **Size:** around 18cm
- **Period:** late Triassic

Icarosaurus This small reptile was able to glide short distances, thanks to a layer of skin supported by a series of very long ribs. This made an airfoil-shaped wing that kept it aloft as it leapt from the tree branches in the lush tropical rainforests.

240 million years ago there were small reptiles which were able to jump and glide through the air.

Spiny back

LONGISQUAMA means 'long scales'.
- **Discovery:** Asia
- **Size:** 15cm
- **Period:** early Triassic

Longisquama Along its backbone there were *two rows of moveable bony plates*, in the form of very long scales. When these were spread out, it was able to float down like a parachute or *glide short distances*, like dragonflies do today.

Placodus and Nothosaurus
Marine reptiles

During the Triassic period there were marine reptiles which hunted in the sea. The Nothosaurus, a later member of this group, evolved with a larger body which was several metres long.

Nothosaurus It is possible that its lifestyle was similar to that of a seal, *hunting in the sea* and living on land. It used its powerful *webbed feet* and its *long tail* to swim. Its *long, sharp teeth* meant it could catch even the quickest fish.

The earliest turtle-like creatures date back to the beginning of the Triassic period but went extinct about 200 million years ago.

Needle teeth

NOTHOSAURUS means 'false reptile'.
- **Discovery:** Europe, North Africa and Asia
- **Size:** around 3m
- **Period:** mid-Triassic

Placodus This reptile had a *crest* along its back. As well as being able to swim, it used its short and sturdy legs to walk on the seabed, and its claws to *scrape* off molluscs clinging to rocks. It had two types of teeth: *prominent teeth* slanting forwards for catching food (clams, mussels and other molluscs) and *flat back teeth*, for grinding.

Flat teeth

PLACODUS belongs to the group of the placodonts ('flat teeth').
- **Discovery:** Central Europe and China
- **Size:** 2m
- **Period:** first half of the Triassic

23

Huge eyes

ICHTHYOSAURUS means 'fish lizard'.
- **Discovery:** Europe
- **Size:** around 2m
- **Period:** appeared at the end of the Triassic period and thrived in the Jurassic period

24

Ichthyosaurus
Dolphin-like

Ichthyosaurus was an excellent swimmer and very well adapted to life in the sea. It gave birth to live young in the water, like whales and dolphins do today.

Ichthyosaurus thrashed its tail when swimming, like modern sharks or tuna fish. It used its fins to change direction and its dorsal fin for balance. It breathed with its lungs by jumping out of the water. Its shape meant that it was very similar to a dolphin in terms of speed. It had large eyes and long jaws with sharp teeth for eating fish, shellfish, molluscs and squid-like creatures.

Judging from its large eyes, the Ichthyosaurus must have had good vision.

Elasmosaurus and Mosasaurus
Other earlier marine reptiles

Elasmosaurus is the longest known marine reptile. The neck alone was more than half of its total length. Mosasaurus had a powerful jaw and the largest ones were three times longer than a male walrus.

Long neck

ELASMOSAURUS means 'thin plate'.
- **Discovery:** Kansas, USA
- **Size:** 14m long, its neck alone being 8m long
- **Period:** late Cretaceous

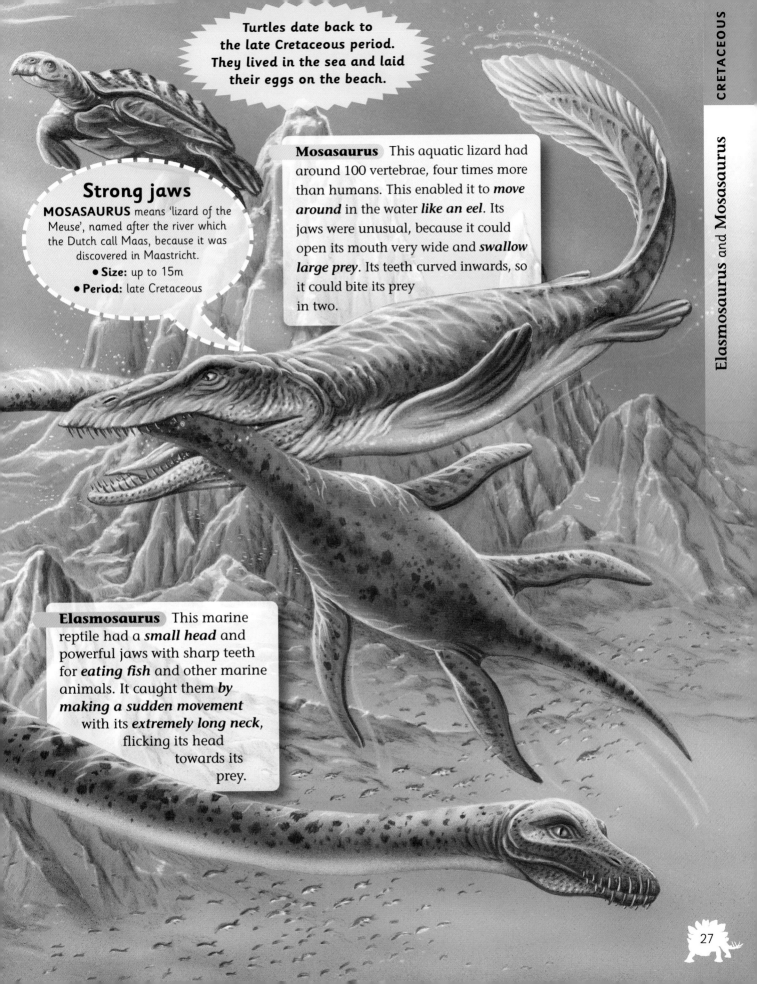

Turtles date back to the late Cretaceous period. They lived in the sea and laid their eggs on the beach.

Elasmosaurus and Mosasaurus

Strong jaws

MOSASAURUS means 'lizard of the Meuse', named after the river which the Dutch call Maas, because it was discovered in Maastricht.

- **Size:** up to 15m
- **Period:** late Cretaceous

Mosasaurus This aquatic lizard had around 100 vertebrae, four times more than humans. This enabled it to **move around** in the water **like an eel**. Its jaws were unusual, because it could open its mouth very wide and **swallow large prey**. Its teeth curved inwards, so it could bite its prey in two.

Elasmosaurus This marine reptile had a **small head** and powerful jaws with sharp teeth for **eating fish** and other marine animals. It caught them **by making a sudden movement** with its **extremely long neck**, flicking its head towards its prey.

Deinosuchus

A really gigantic crocodile

The biggest crocodile of all time, reaching anywhere between 12 to 15m long, was around at the same time as dinosaurs and no doubt ate some of them!

Meat eater

DEINOSUCHUS means 'terrible crocodile'.

- **Discovery:** USA
- **Size:** 12 to 15m long
- **Period:** late Cretaceous

This Deinosuchus was capable of attacking and eating a dinosaur such as Triceratops.

Deinosuchus This is the biggest crocodile ever discovered. Its legs were larger than those of a modern crocodile. Its enormous size and *powerful* jaw meant it could attack certain dinosaurs when they were paddling in the water.

PTEROSAURS

These winged reptiles were the first vertebrates designed to fly. They lived alongside dinosaurs from the Triassic period until the Cretaceous period and became extinct with them. They came in all kinds of different shapes and sizes.

Quetzalcoatlus had narrow, yet extremely long wings.

Quetzalcoatlus One of the *last pterosaurs*, found in the north of Mexico and the south of Texas. At that time, this area was similar to the modern wetlands and lakes along tropical coasts. It had a *very long neck and beak* and large toothless jaws, which suggests it ate fish or carrion (dead animals).

Quetzalcoatlus

Bigger than a small aeroplane

The Quetzalcoatlus was the largest flying animal ever to have existed. When its wings were spread, its wingspan was up to 15m.

Feathered serpent

QUETZALCOATLUS was named after the Aztec god Quetzalcoatl, which means 'feathered serpent'.
- **Size:** wingspan of 12 to 15m
- **Period:** late Cretaceous

Pteranodon

A flying reptile with a crest

The Pteranodon was characterised by its long beak with a pouch and its big crest, which may have balanced it during flight.

Winged and toothless

PTERANODON means 'winged and toothless'.

- **Discovery:** Kansas, USA and England
- **Size:** wingspan of around 9m
- **Period:** late Cretaceous

Pteranodon Like marine birds, the Pteranodon ate fish. Its **long beak** was used to scoop up fish as it flew just above the surface of the sea. The **large crest** on the upper part of its head acted as a **counterweight** to balance out the weight of the beak and the fish.

Pteranodon stored fish in the pouch under its beak, just like pelicans do today.

DINOSAURS

Dinosaurs were land reptiles from the Triassic, Jurassic and Cretaceous periods. They were different from primitive reptiles because they were able to walk and run with their legs extended directly beneath their bodies, rather than at their sides. They mysteriously disappeared at the end of the Cretaceous period, 65 million years ago.

The smallest dinosaurs

Not all dinosaurs were huge and heavy. There were also small species like Compsognathus, which was no more than 60cm long and only around 2.5kg when fully grown.

Even smaller skeletons have been discovered, but they all belonged to young dinosaurs. We know this because their skulls and legs are very big compared to their bodies.

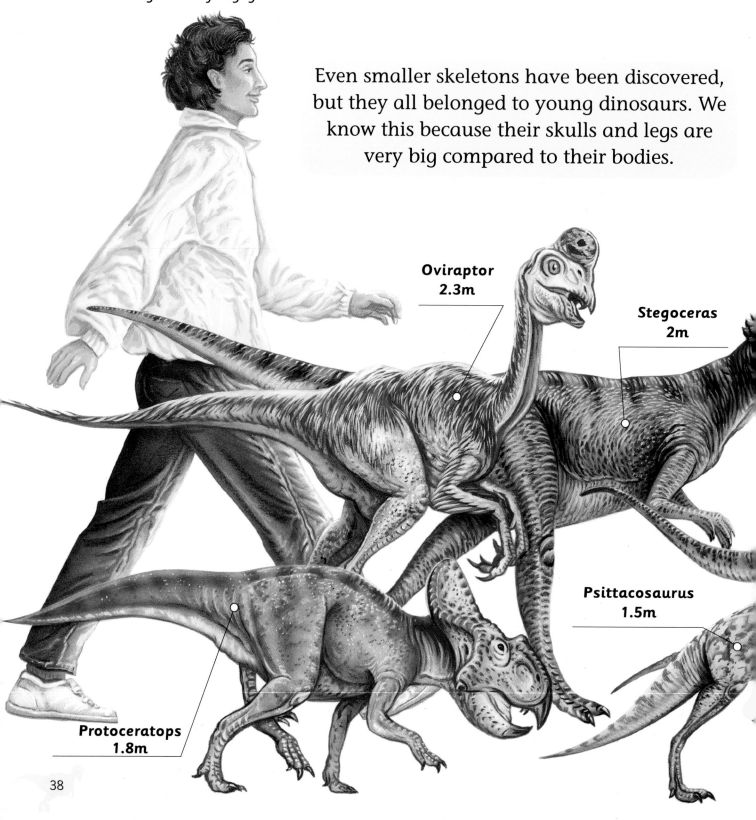

Oviraptor
2.3m

Stegoceras
2m

Psittacosaurus
1.5m

Protoceratops
1.8m

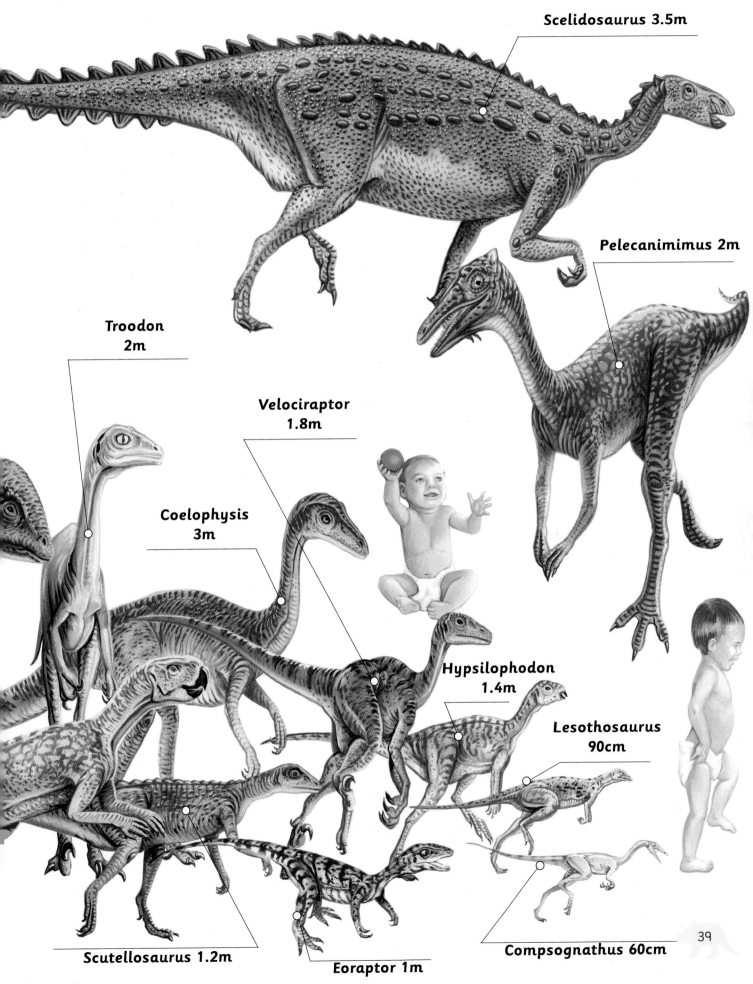

Scelidosaurus 3.5m

Pelecanimimus 2m

Troodon
2m

Velociraptor
1.8m

Coelophysis
3m

Hypsilophodon
1.4m

Lesothosaurus
90cm

Scutellosaurus 1.2m

Eoraptor 1m

Compsognathus 60cm

39

The biggest dinosaurs

The biggest species could reach up to 35m from their head to the tip of their long tail. There is only one animal alive today which is similar in size: the blue whale, which is almost 30m long and can weigh around 150 tons.

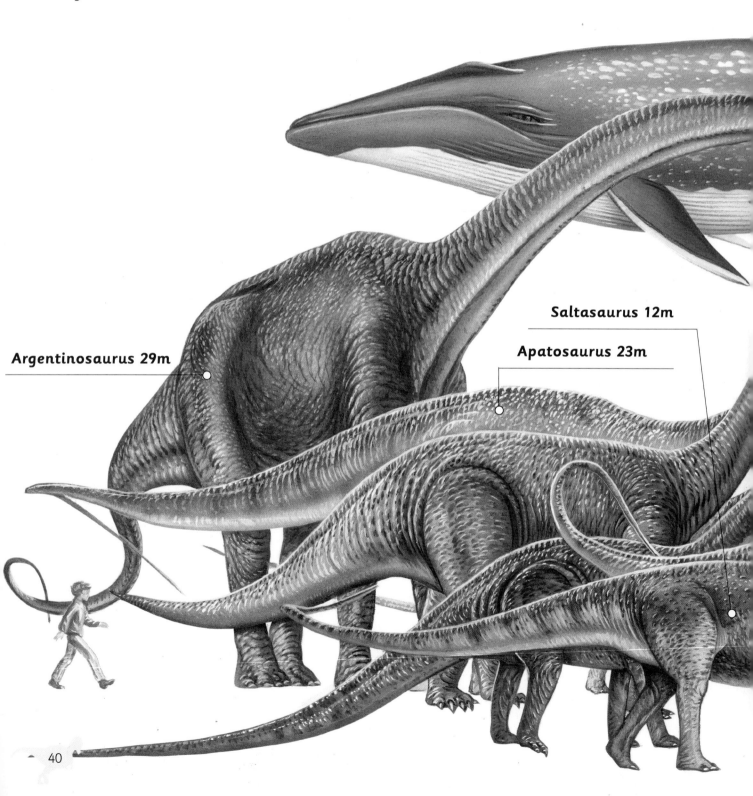

Saltasaurus 12m

Apatosaurus 23m

Argentinosaurus 29m

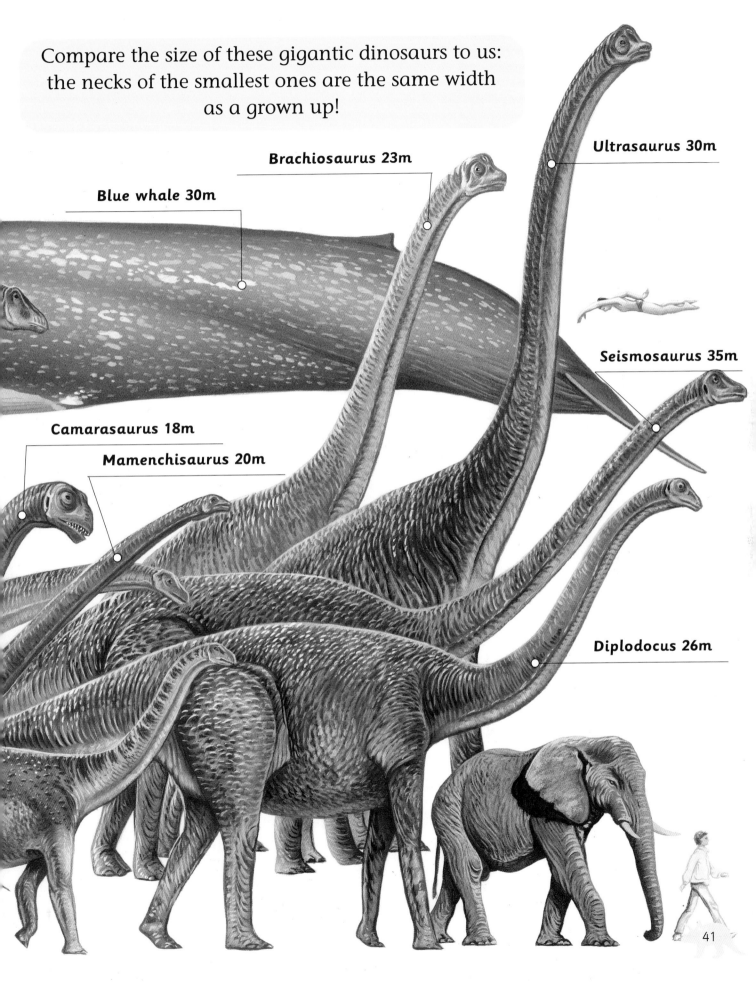

Compare the size of these gigantic dinosaurs to us: the necks of the smallest ones are the same width as a grown up!

Blue whale 30m

Brachiosaurus 23m

Ultrasaurus 30m

Seismosaurus 35m

Camarasaurus 18m

Mamenchisaurus 20m

Diplodocus 26m

Two types of dinosaur

Dinosaurs are divided into two groups: Saurischia and Ornithischia. The hip bones of saurischian dinosaurs were separate, whilst the hip bones of ornithischian dinosaurs were connected and slanted backwards. This determined how they walked.

The carnivorous saurischian dinosaurs walked on two legs and the enormous herbivores, with their column-like legs, walked on all four. All of the ornithischian dinosaurs walked on all fours and were herbivores.

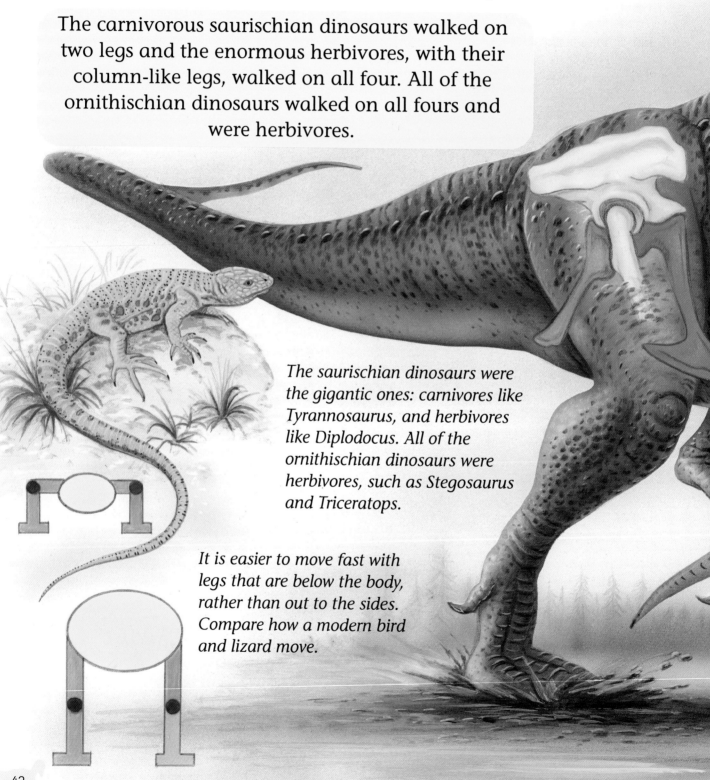

The saurischian dinosaurs were the gigantic ones: carnivores like Tyrannosaurus, and herbivores like Diplodocus. All of the ornithischian dinosaurs were herbivores, such as Stegosaurus and Triceratops.

It is easier to move fast with legs that are below the body, rather than out to the sides. Compare how a modern bird and lizard move.

A carnivorous saurischian dinosaur: Allosaurus

An ornithischian dinosaur (all herbivores): Iguanodon

Herrerasaurus Could be up to **4m long** and **2m tall**. It could weigh 300kg. It had a **powerful jaw** with rows of small teeth for eating its prey, which it caught with the **claws** on its short, strong front legs.

Early dinosaur

HERRERASAURUS means 'Herrera's lizard', named after the man who discovered it.
- **Size:** About 3m long
- **Period:** middle Triassic

Herrerasaurus was a primitive dinosaur, but a deadly predator.

Eoraptor and Herrerasaurus
A pair of fast runners

These were some of the earliest dinosaurs to inhabit Earth. They walked on their two hind legs, raising their tail when running to balance out the front section of their body. This allowed them to reach high speeds.

Grasping hands

EORAPTOR means 'dawn thief'.
- **Discovery**: Valley of the Moon, a desert in Argentina
- **Period**: late Triassic

Eoraptor Thought to be the *most primitive* dinosaur ever discovered. It was only 1m long, but it was a *skilled hunter* which ate mammals, small lizards and insects. It chased its prey on its two *fast hind legs*.

45

Plateosaurus
The earliest large herbivorous dinosaur

This was the first land animal to be able to reach tall vegetation to eat. It was one of the earliest dinosaur discoveries, with fossils found in France in 1837. Its remains are common in Europe and over 100 skeletons have been found.

These flying reptiles seem to be scared by the size of the Plateosaurus.

Plateosaurus Capable of standing on four legs or two, Plateosaurus could eat either low-growing plants or foliage from trees higher up. Its hands had *strong fingers*, particularly the thumb, which had a *wide claw* which it used to tear leaves from trees or to defend itself.

Mystery name

PLATEOSAURUS means 'flat lizard' but no-one is sure why it was given that name!

- **Size:** 6 to 8m
- **Period:** late Triassic

47

Stegosaurus
A dinosaur with plates on its back

The two lines of plates on its back regulated its temperature.
Stegosaurus roamed through plains eating low-growing
vegetation. It was as heavy as a rhinoceros and as
long as a bus.

The Stegosaurus had
giant spikes on the end of
its tail for warding
off enemies.

Tiny brain

STEGOSAURUS means 'roof lizard'.
- **Size:** up to 9m long,
  2 tons in weight.
- **Period:** late Jurassic

Stegosaurus A herbivore living in North America, Asia, Africa and Europe. Its brain was as tiny as a walnut and its *small head* ended in a beak. It had *two rows of plates* on its back, supplied with blood which *cooled down its body* whilst it was digesting the enormous quantity of plants it ate.

Allosaurus
The most fearful carnivorous animal

Allosaurus ate herbivorous dinosaurs of various sizes. An Allosaurus could not tackle large prey, like Stegosaurus, on its own, but would look for weaker targets, such as young, elderly or ill animals.

These two young Stegosaurus have already learnt to use their tails to defend themselves from the Allosaurus.

Allosaurus One of the most ferocious dinosaurs of North America, and the **most common** large carnivore. It walked **on two legs** and caught its prey with its **three claws** whilst choking it with **its jaws**. It had small crests on its head.

Fierce giant
ALLOSAURUS means 'different lizard'.
• **Size:** around 9m long and 3m tall
• **Period:** late Jurassic

51

Ceratosaurus This great hunter had enormous jaws and *curved, sharp teeth*. Its front legs were short with *four toes*. Characterised by the *horn on its snout*, it is possible that the males used it as a weapon when fighting over females.

Ridged head

CERATOSAURUS means 'horned lizard'.
- **Discovery:** Morrison Formation, USA
- **Size:** up to 6m long and 2m tall
- **Period:** late Jurassic

Ceratosaurus

Another carnivore with powerful jaws

Ceratosaurus lived alongside Allosaurus, Apatosaurus, Diplodocus and Stegosaurus in North America. It may well have hunted the same prey as Allosaurus, but it was smaller, more agile and lighter than its competitor.

These Ceratosaurus may be fighting over a female.

53

Diplodocus
A powerful, whip-like tail

Diplodocus is one of the most well-known dinosaurs. It was a very large, four-legged animal with a long neck and tail. The end of its tail was very thin, which meant it may have been used as a whip for self-defence.

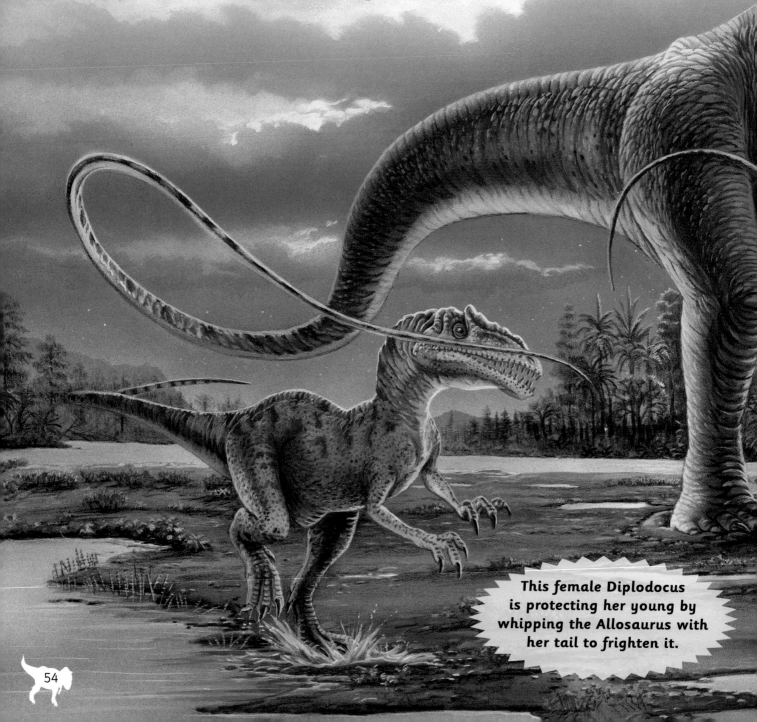

This female Diplodocus is protecting her young by whipping the Allosaurus with her tail to frighten it.

Diplodocus Had a *very long tail and neck* and four *sturdy legs*. Its head was tiny compared to the size of its body which was

more than 20m in length, half of which was its tail. *It ate leaves and seeds* from tall trees and bushes, as well as ferns and vegetation from the ground.

Double bones

DIPLODOCUS means 'double beam', named after the bones in its tail.

- **Discovery:** Morrison Formation, USA
- **Size:** up to 27m long and more than 10 tons in weight
- **Period:** late Jurassic

55

Apatosaurus Very *similar to Diplodocus* which it lived with in North America. It had *a thicker neck*, its sturdy legs were even larger and its extremely long neck had more vertebrae, which meant that the Apatosaurus was *three times heavier*. Its legs had short toes, like an elephant. It was also a *herbivore* and moved slowly because of its weight, and *lived in herds* for protection.

Nostrils on top

APATOSAURUS means 'deceptive lizard'.
- **Discovery:** Morrison Formation, USA
- **Size:** around 25m long
- **Period:** late Jurassic

Apatosaurus
Elephant-like legs and a long tail

Apatosaurus was a grazing animal which lived in herds. Like the Diplodocus, it had an elongated neck and a very long whip-like tail which acted as a counterweight. Its sturdy legs were like those of an elephant, but with clawed feet.

Long back legs

BRACHIOSAURUS means 'arm lizard'.

- **Discovery:** Morrison Formation, USA
- **Size:** up to 13m tall and 25m long
- **Period:** late Jurassic

Brachiosaurus This sauropod lived in herds in North America, Europe, Asia and Africa, and *weighed more than 70 tons*. It *walked on four legs* and had a *long neck*, which was adapted to reach tree canopies for food. Its tail was comparatively short.

Brachiosaurus

A gigantic giraffe

This gigantic herbivore is the heaviest and tallest dinosaur ever to have lived on dry land. Like giraffes, its long neck and long legs enabled it to reach tree canopies.

It is thought that Brachiosaurus had a reasonably large and strong heart which could pump blood all the way to its head.

59

Archaeopteryx and Ornitholestes
The earliest bird and the bird robber

Archaeopteryx existed 150 million years ago and is the earliest known bird. We still don't know whether it was truly a bird or a dinosaur, because it shared characteristics with both. Ornitholestes was a fast, carnivorous dinosaur which may have eaten birds.

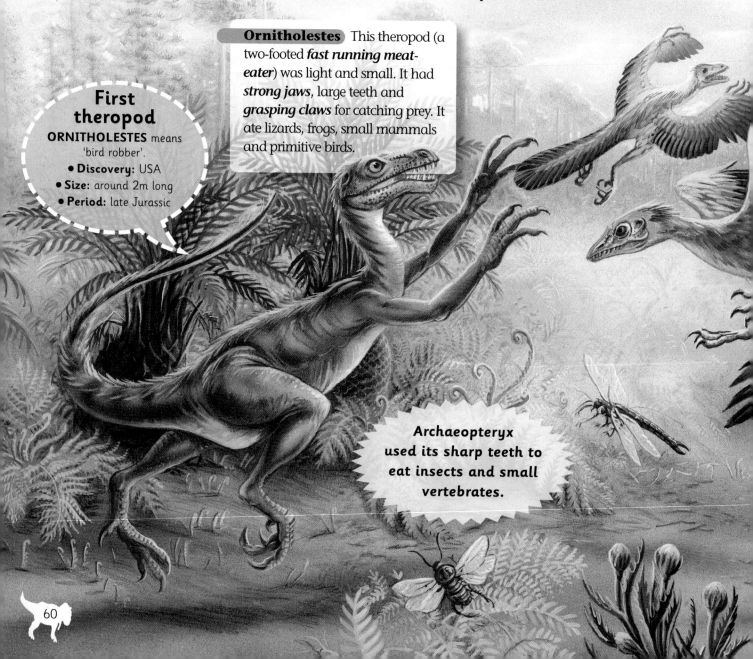

Ornitholestes This theropod (a two-footed *fast running meat-eater*) was light and small. It had *strong jaws*, large teeth and *grasping claws* for catching prey. It ate lizards, frogs, small mammals and primitive birds.

First theropod
ORNITHOLESTES means 'bird robber'.
• **Discovery:** USA
• **Size:** around 2m long
• **Period:** late Jurassic

Archaeopteryx used its sharp teeth to eat insects and small vertebrates.

Archaeopteryx This animal was *in between reptiles and birds*. Like dinosaurs, it had *teeth, clawed* hands and a *long hollow tail*; like birds, it had *feathers and wings*, which enabled it to glide from one tree to another.

Original bird

ARCHAEOPTERYX means 'ancient wing'.

• **Discovery:** Southern Germany
• **Size:** between 35 and 60cm long
• **Period:** late Jurassic

61

Baryonyx This dinosaur had crocodile-like jaws and *many teeth*, suggesting that it ate fish. It had *very sharp claws* on three of the toes on its front legs. It is thought that it would lie in wait on river banks and use its claws to *catch fish*.

Baryonyx
Cretaceous fish-eater

Its jaws and teeth suggest that the Baryonyx was an animal which mainly ate fish. One specimen was found with fish bones and scales inside its body. It may have fished from the riverbank, like a grizzly bear.

Baryonyx lived in warm and humid areas with lots of rivers and lakes.

Fish catcher

BARYONYX means 'heavy claw'.
- **Discovery:** Southern England, northern Spain
- **Size:** 9m long and around 5m tall
- **Period:** early Cretaceous

Herbivorous dinosaurs

Most dinosaurs were herbivores. At that time there was a lot of vegetation, so there was enough food for everyone. The young dinosaurs nibbled on soft shoots and plants on the ground. The teeth and snout of each dinosaur were designed to cut, tear or chew their favourite plants.

Iguanodon
Used its beak to bite leaves, then crushed them with its back teeth, which were like those of an iguana, only bigger.

Hypsilophodon
Small in size, it would have eaten low-growing vegetation, using its beak to nibble shoots, and its chisel-shaped teeth to chew them.

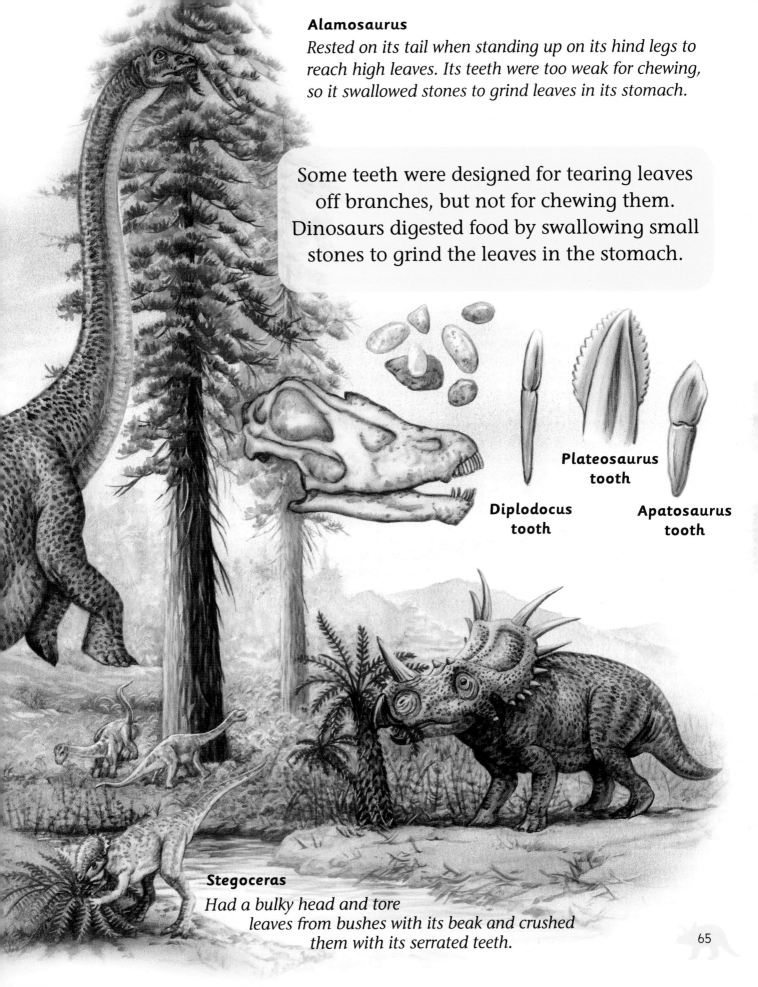

Alamosaurus

Rested on its tail when standing up on its hind legs to reach high leaves. Its teeth were too weak for chewing, so it swallowed stones to grind leaves in its stomach.

Some teeth were designed for tearing leaves off branches, but not for chewing them. Dinosaurs digested food by swallowing small stones to grind the leaves in the stomach.

Diplodocus tooth

Plateosaurus tooth

Apatosaurus tooth

Stegoceras

Had a bulky head and tore leaves from bushes with its beak and crushed them with its serrated teeth.

Iguanodon
The most common Cretaceous herbivore

Lots of fossils of this dinosaur have been discovered in European archaeological sites. The tip of its powerful jaw was a beak and it had lots of molars which meant it could chew plants.

This Iguanodon is defending itself from a carnivorous dinosaur by brandishing its thumb spike.

Horny beak

IGUANODON *means 'iguana tooth'.*
- **Discovery:** England, Belgium, Germany, Africa, USA
- **Size:** 10m long
- **Period:** early Cretaceous

Iguanodon Many of its fossils have been found in the same location, which leads us to believe it *lived in herds*, on fertile plains where it *ate trees and fern*. It could walk on two or four legs, since it had hoof-like claws. The thumbs of its hands had a *sharp spike* which was used for self-defence.

If an attacker was very big, like this Carcharodontosaurus, there was no choice but to run.

Ouranosaurus
Hoofs and a crest

Like its relative Iguanodon, Ouranosaurus was a herbivore. It was characterised by the crest on its back, which was for regulating its temperature. It could walk on either two or four legs, because it also had claws that were hoof-shaped.

Ouranosaurus Like the Iguanodon, it had a *thumb spike* for self-defence, but it was smaller. It was different from the Iguanodon in that it had a crest which covered its back and part of its tail. This was for *controlling its body temperature*, and perhaps also for identifying one another and for attracting a partner, because it lived in *herds*.

Long snout
OURANOSAURUS means 'brave lizard'.
- **Discovery:** Niger, Africa
- **Size:** around 7m in length and around 4 tons in weight
- **Period:** mid-Cretaceous

Amargasaurus
A dinosaur with a crest and spines

The two rows of spines covering its back must have been a good weapon of defence against attacking carnivores. It may have had a single or double strip of skin between the spines, running all the way down to the tail, forming a crest.

Brandishing its spikes, this Amargasaurus is defending its young from an attacking carnosaur.

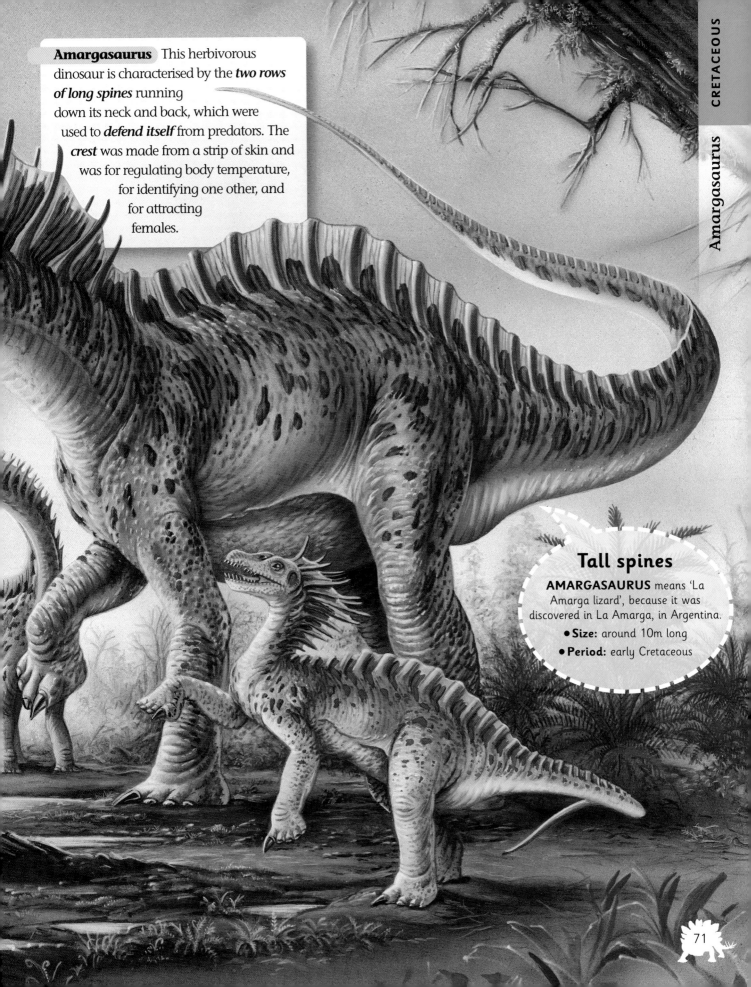

Amargasaurus This herbivorous dinosaur is characterised by the *two rows of long spines* running down its neck and back, which were used to *defend itself* from predators. The *crest* was made from a strip of skin and was for regulating body temperature, for identifying one other, and for attracting females.

Tall spines

AMARGASAURUS means 'La Amarga lizard', because it was discovered in La Amarga, in Argentina.

- **Size:** around 10m long
- **Period:** early Cretaceous

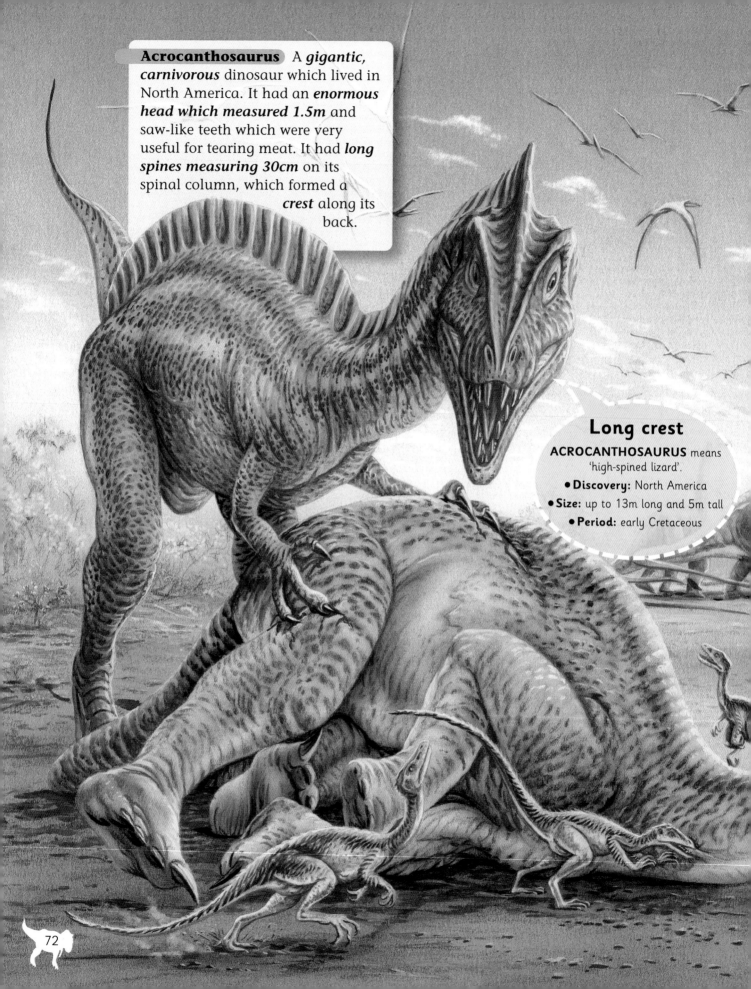

Acrocanthosaurus A *gigantic, carnivorous* dinosaur which lived in North America. It had an *enormous head which measured 1.5m* and saw-like teeth which were very useful for tearing meat. It had *long spines measuring 30cm* on its spinal column, which formed a *crest* along its back.

Long crest

ACROCANTHOSAURUS means 'high-spined lizard'.
• **Discovery:** North America
• **Size:** up to 13m long and 5m tall
• **Period:** early Cretaceous

Acrocanthosaurus

A ferocious carnivore

Judging from its large size and enormous head, this must have been a very ferocious carnivore. It had a crest on its back which was 30cm tall, running from its head to its tail.

Acrocanthosaurus needed to catch large prey to satisfy its appetite.

73

Spinosaurus
A dinosaur with a sail

Its very tall crest could be up to over 1.5m high. It worked as a solar panel to provide heat, or a 'sail' to cool the dinosaur down using the wind. Seventeen metres in length, it is the largest known carnivore (even bigger than Tyrannosaurus and Carcharodontosaurus).

Enormous

SPINOSAURUS means 'spine lizard'.
Discovery: Egypt and Morocco, Africa
- **Size:** 17m long and 5m tall
- **Period:** mid-Cretaceous

Spinosaurus easily conquered prey with its vicious claws and teeth.

Spinosaurus Its jaws were long like those of a crocodile. *It walked on two legs* using the front ones to catch its prey. Despite its size, it was *quite light*, which meant it was good at hunting fish and dinosaurs. Its *enormous sail* heated up very quickly in the sun, and when Spinosaurus stood against the wind, its body temperature decreased.

Psittacosaurus
Dinosaur with a parrot-like beak

It is named after the shape of its snout, which was very similar to the curved beak of a parrot. It is the first known dinosaur to have developed this kind of beak in order to eat plants with tough leaves.

Tough beak
PSITTACOSAURUS means 'parrot lizard'.
- **Discovery:** Asia
- **Size:** 2m long
- **Period:** early-Cretaceous

Psittacosaurus ground food in its stomach by swallowing stones.

Psittacosaurus Lived at a time when the first plants with flowers were appearing and it is possible that it used its **strong curved beak** to cut through their tough leaves. It was **small in size** and when it stood up to grab branches, it was almost the same height as a human being.

Duck beaks

Duck-billed dinosaurs had very wide beaks, like those of a duck. They lived in herds for better protection against predators. It is possible that they inhabited leafy forests and marshlands.

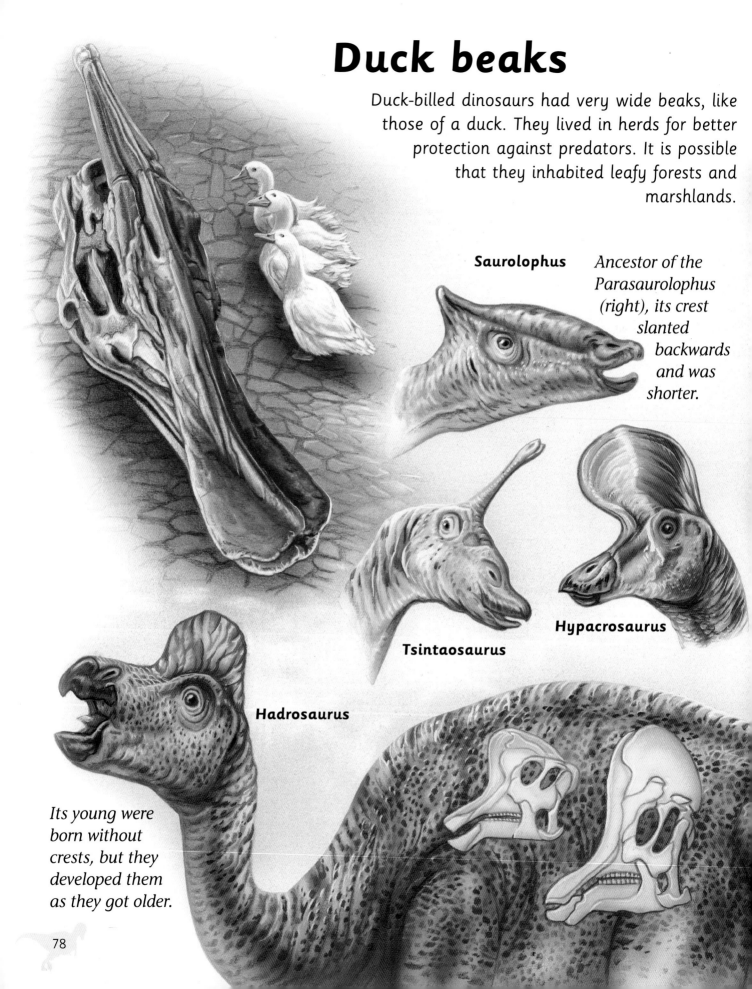

Saurolophus Ancestor of the Parasaurolophus (right), its crest slanted backwards and was shorter.

Tsintaosaurus

Hypacrosaurus

Hadrosaurus

Its young were born without crests, but they developed them as they got older.

Parasaurolophus

Skull of a male Parasaurolophus

Skull of a female Parasaurolophus

The inside of their crest was hollow, with tubes. It is believed that the crest was a sound box used for communicating with each other.

Lambeosaurus

Kritosaurus

The Protohadros was discovered in Texas and is the earliest known hadrosaur.

Maiasaura

Edmontosaurus

Protohadros

Parasaurolophus
Trombone noises

This is one of the most striking duck-beaked dinosaurs. It had a large crest in the form of a tube which curved backwards from the snout and could be up to 1.8m long. It may have been able to use this crest to make bellowing sounds which could be heard far away.

Hollow crest

PARASAUROLOPHUS means 'near crested lizard'.
- **Discovery:** North America
- **Size:** up to 12m long
- **Period:** late Cretaceous

Parasaurolophus warned its companions of danger by bellowing with its crest.

Parasaurolophus This dinosaur lived in herds, and used its *tubed crest* to make *bellowing noises* like a trombone to communicate with others in its group, and to identify one another. Females had a smaller crest. It could walk on either *four or two legs*, which meant it could eat tall or low plants, with its *wide, duck-like beak*.

Oviraptor
The egg thief?

Fossils of this animal have been found next to nests full of eggs, and it was thought that Oviraptor was an egg-eating dinosaur. This gave it the name 'egg thief'. It has since been suggested that the dinosaur was actually sitting on top of its own nest, to hatch and protect the eggs.

The feathers, beaks and bones of the Oviraptor lead us to believe that it was an animal somewhere between a dinosaur and a bird.

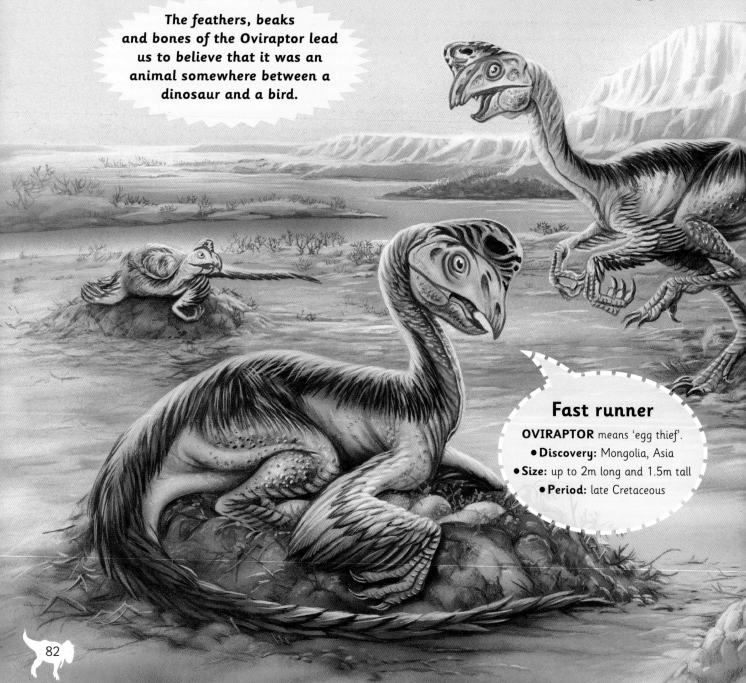

Fast runner

OVIRAPTOR means 'egg thief'.
- **Discovery:** Mongolia, Asia
- **Size:** up to 2m long and 1.5m tall
- **Period:** late Cretaceous

Oviraptor If this dinosaur did eat eggs, its *curved, toothless beak* would have allowed it to crack them open whilst holding them with its front legs. Alternatively, Oviraptor may have eaten meat, seeds and insects. It was a *small, speedy creature* with a crest, and *feathers* on its back, front legs and tail.

Dinosaurs or birds?

There were animals which were somewhere in between dinosaurs and birds: they had feathers, wing-like structures, and bird-like feet, but their teeth and bony tails belonged to a dinosaur.

The Archaeopteryx could be the missing link in the evolutionary chain between dinosaurs and modern birds.

Oviraptor

As well as having feathers, its collar bone was similar to that of a modern bird, but it couldn't fly.

Caudipteryx

Its name means 'tail feather'. Although it couldn't fly, it was able to glide from one tree to another, or flap its wings to scare away its enemy.

Sinornithosaurus

Also discovered in China and even though it looked like a bird, it couldn't fly. Its arms and hands were very long in comparison to its body.

Beipiaosaurus

More than 2m long, this is the largest known feathered dinosaur. It was discovered in China.

Archaeopteryx

With its wings, feathers and collar bone, it looked like a bird. It could flap its wings and jump short distances when hunting small vertebrates.

Camouflage

We can't tell what colour dinosaurs were from looking at fossils, but if we look at modern animals we can get quite a good idea.

Dinosaurs appear to have come in lots of different colours, just like animals do today.

Iguanodon might have been green in order to camouflage itself in ferny forests.

Hypsilophodon may even have been able to change colour, like a chameleon.

Striped, like a tiger?

The crest of Corythosaurus may have been different colours and used for display, like a modern cockatoo.

Green, like a lizard?

Most dinosaur pictures are an artist's impression, based on facts that are known, such as the animal's habitat and lifestyle. Velociraptor may have been camouflaged or even covered with feathers.

Deinonychus and Tenontosaurus
Little conquers large

Deinonychus was a ferocious carnivore with a scary, curved claw. Since it hunted in groups, it was able to attack Tenontosaurus which was double its size.

Tenontosaurus With its *stout, stocky body*, it needed muscular legs to carry its weight of around 1 ton. It didn't have sharp teeth but it had molars for *chewing leaves*. It defended itself using its *long, powerful tail*.

This Tenontosaurus doesn't have any weapons for defending itself from the group attack of Deinonychus.

Deinonychus Lived in herds and *hunted in groups* in order to kill animals much bigger than itself. It used its good vision to locate prey from far away and then darted towards them with its tail upright. It launched itself onto its prey, gripping it with its *long arms* whilst keeping enough distance to lift its foot and *pierce it with its sickle-shaped claw*. It used its teeth, which slanted inwards, to tear the meat.

Killer claw
DEINONYCHUS means 'terrible claw'.
- **Discovery:** Montana, USA
- **Size:** around 3m long
- **Period:** first half of the Cretaceous

Strong tail
TENONTOSAURUS means 'sinew lizard'.
- **Discovery:** Wyoming and Montana, USA
- **Size:** up to 7m long and 2.5m tall
- **Period:** First half of the Cretaceous

Barrel shaped

PROTOCERATOPS means 'first horned face'.
- **Discovery:** Mongolia, Asia
- **Size:** 2m long
- **Period:** late Cretaceous

Protoceratops It had a *small and heavy* body, and walked on all four legs. It had a bony shield around its neck which, along with its *beak*, protected it from being attacked by carnivores. Even though it looked ferocious, it only *ate plants*.

Velociraptor It was very similar to Deinonychus, although it was smaller. It *ran quickly* with its tail upright so it could change direction suddenly, and kept the *long curved claw* on each foot raised to avoid damaging it, since it was needed *for killing* prey.

Small killer

VELOCIRAPTOR means 'swift seizer'.
- **Discovery:** Mongolia and China
- **Size:** 1.8m long
- **Period:** late Cretaceous

Velociraptor and Protoceratops
Group attack

Velociraptor was a fast and fearful carnivore when it hunted in groups. Protoceratops, which was the same size but much heavier, could only defend itself with its enormous beak and the large shield around its neck.

The first dinosaur eggs ever discovered came from Protoceratops and this is why it is so well-known.

91

Enormous heads with horns

There were three main families of horned dinosaurs. They were all herbivores and had impressive plates of bone around their necks. These may have been for frightening enemies or for attracting females and fighting over them with other males of the species, using their impressive set of horns.

**Torosaurus
7.5m long**

**Pentaceratops
6m long**

The skull of Torosaurus was 13 times the size of a human one, but its brain was smaller, its skull being full of muscle and bone instead.

A complete skeleton of Triceratops has never been found but from the large number of skulls and horns discovered, it seems to be one of the most common horned dinosaurs of its time.

Bagaceratops **Protoceratops** **Centrosaurus** **Triceratops**

Triceratops 9m long

Triceratops was one of the last horned dinosaurs to live on Earth. It looked a bit like a gigantic rhinoceros.

Chasmosaurus The rectangular *bony plate* on its neck wasn't solid bone, but muscle covered with skin. Although it had small horns around it, *it was only for show and for scaring off enemies*. It had sharp horns above its eyes and on its nose. It is thought that males fighting over a female would lock their front horns, like stags.

Charge at the enemy

CHASMOSAURUS means 'opening lizard'.
- **Discovery:** Alberta, Canada
- **Size:** up to 8m long
- **Period:** late Cretaceous

Chasmosaurus

The earliest horned dinosaur with a bony plate

This dinosaur's name refers to the large openings in its neck frill. It was a herbivore and lived in groups for protection. When carnivores saw its impressive bony plates and horns pointing towards them, they wouldn't dare attack.

Despite its appearance, Chasmosaurus only ate plants, which it tore with its curved beak.

Pentaceratops
Five horns or three?

When its skull was discovered, it was believed to have had five horns: two on the forehead, one on the nose and two on either side; but it was later discovered that the two side horns were just an extension of its protruding cheeks.

Huge skull

PENTACERATOPS means 'five-horned face'.
- **Discovery:** New Mexico, USA
- **Size:** up to 8m long
- **Period:** late Cretaceous

Pentaceratops It defended itself with its *long horns* which pointed forwards. The edge of its *bony plate, with small horns*, provided extra defence against predators trying to bite its neck. When its head was lowered, the plate remained upright and the animal looked even more threatening. It *grazed* amongst low-growing plants, which it bit with its powerful *beak*. It had *muscular legs*, similar to those of a rhinoceros.

Two male Pentaceratops fighting over a female, locking horns.

97

Triceratops and Therizinosaurus

Biggest horns fights against longest claws

Triceratops was the dinosaur with the biggest and most powerful horns. It lived at the same time as Therizinosaurus, which had extremely long claws (over 70cm).

Triceratops Lived in herds and only attacked to defend itself. It had *two horns* on its forehead *which were up to 1m long* and another small horn on its snout. It walked on all four feet; the front ones were very strong, to carry the weight of its *head, which measured 2 to 3m.* It had a bony *plate* which protected its neck. It ate plants, which it cut with its *beak*.

Running is the best option when faced with the claws of Therizinosaurus, even with a Triceratops' defences!

Armoured beast

TRICERATOPS means 'three-horned face'.
- **Discovery:** North America
- **Size:** 9m long
- **Period:** late Cretaceous

Therizinosaurus Very little is known about this dinosaur, because not all of its bones have been discovered. Fossils do reveal its enormous *front claws*, which may have been used to shake very high trees so it could eat the leaves, or perhaps for self-defence.

Scary sight
THERIZINOSAURUS means 'scythe lizard', named after its enormous claws.
- **Discovery:** Mongolia, Asia
- **Size:** up to 12m long
- **Period:** late Cretaceous

Saichania Its head and whole body were covered with a *bony shield full of spikes* for protection. It had a *heavy club* on the end of its tail, which it used to attack its enemies.

Prickly beast
SAICHANIA was called 'beautiful one' because of its well-preserved skeleton.
- **Discovery:** Mongolia, Asia
- **Size:** 7m long
- **Period:** late Cretaceous

This Saichania can defend itself from Tarbosaurus with its tail, even though the other dinosaur is bigger and more ferocious.

Tarbosaurus and Saichania

Large jaws versus a clubbed tail

Tarbosaurus was related to Tyrannosaurus. It had large jaws and was capable of running on two legs so it could jump on its prey. However, the Saichania was able to club it with its tail.

Tarbosaurus From the tyrannosaurid family, but with *more teeth* and a *lighter body* than Tyrannosaurus. With its jaws open wide, it would have been *terrifying*. Its arms and hands were very small and useless for combat, but the powerful *claws on its legs* would have enabled it to knock down its prey.

Tiny arms
TARBOSAURUS means 'alarming lizard'.
- **Discovery:** Mongolia, Asia
- **Size:** between 10 and 12m long and around 5 to 5.5 tons in weight
- **Period:** late Cretaceous

Stygimoloch
Stag-horned dinosaurs

This thick-skulled dinosaur may have used its horns to scare off carnivorous dinosaurs, and for power fighting within its own herd. However, its best weapon of defence was running away, because it was very agile. Some scientists believe it was not a separate species but that the remains found are those of Pachycephalosaurus young.

Stygimoloch ate plants, fruits, seeds and possibly insects.

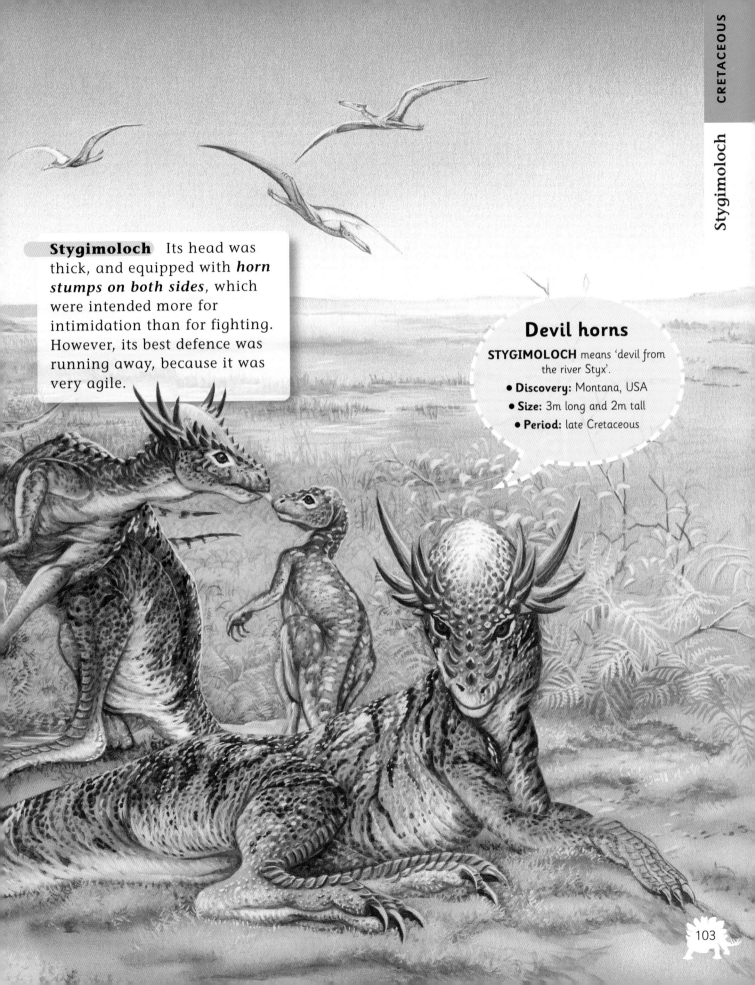

Stygimoloch Its head was thick, and equipped with *horn stumps on both sides*, which were intended more for intimidation than for fighting. However, its best defence was running away, because it was very agile.

Devil horns

STYGIMOLOCH means 'devil from the river Styx'.
- **Discovery:** Montana, USA
- **Size:** 3m long and 2m tall
- **Period:** late Cretaceous

Troodon
The most intelligent dinosaur?

This dinosaur was known as Stenonychosaurus for years. Its brain was very big compared to most dinosaurs. This would have made it roughly as smart as a modern-day bird, which is much cleverer than the large, plant eating dinosaurs.

One scientist has wondered what would happen if Troodon survived extinction...could it have evolved into a 'Dinosauroid' with some human characteristics?

Troodon It had a long neck, *large eyes*, long, narrow jaws with small, sharp teeth, front legs with *three narrow claws* and long hind legs suitable for running.
Due to the *large size of its brain*, it is believed to have had very good vision and a good memory.

Fossil tooth

TROODON means 'wounding tooth'.
- **Discovery:** North America
  Size: 2m long
- **Period:** late Cretaceous

105

Tyrannosaurus
Enormous carnivorous dinosaur

One of the largest of the carnivorous dinosaurs, its head
alone measured more than 1.5m and its enormous
mouth was full of sharp, 20cm-long teeth.
Its body was heavy and was 14m long.

Tyrannosaurus With its heavy body and a solid head, its large jaws measured 1.2m and were full of sharp, curved teeth, which it used to kill its prey by charging against it with its mouth open wide and beating it with its thick and muscular neck. It is possible that it was a scavenger, eating the kills of other creatures.

Dinosaur king

TYRANNOSAURUS means 'tyrant lizard'; Rex means 'king'.
- **Discovery:** USA, Canada, Mongolia
- **Size:** up to 14m long and 6m tall
- **Period:** late Cretaceous

107

Two large carnivores

Enormous and powerful, these two meat-eaters could tear their victims to shreds in seconds with their huge jaws and teeth.

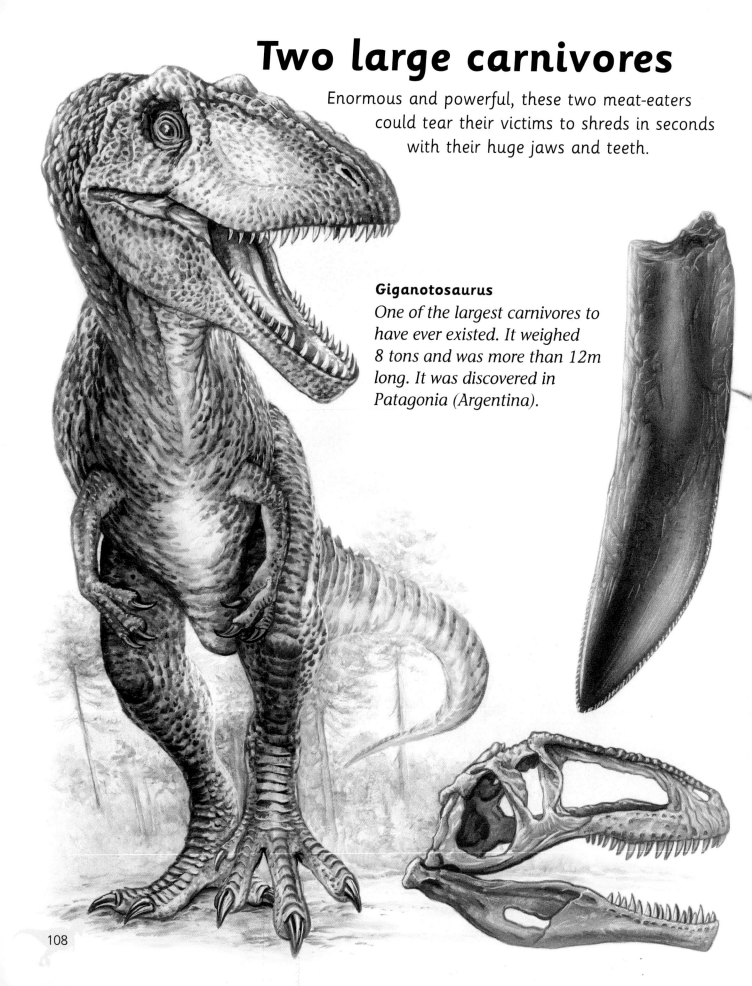

Giganotosaurus

One of the largest carnivores to have ever existed. It weighed 8 tons and was more than 12m long. It was discovered in Patagonia (Argentina).

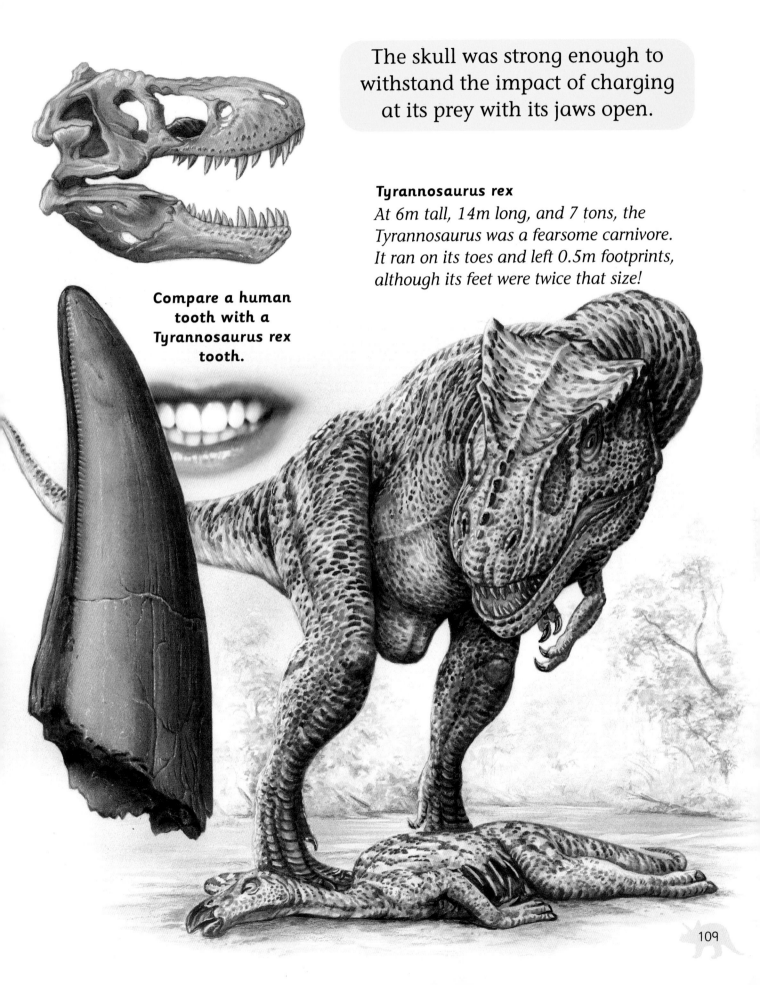

The skull was strong enough to withstand the impact of charging at its prey with its jaws open.

Tyrannosaurus rex

At 6m tall, 14m long, and 7 tons, the Tyrannosaurus was a fearsome carnivore. It ran on its toes and left 0.5m footprints, although its feet were twice that size!

Compare a human tooth with a Tyrannosaurus rex tooth.

SCIENTIFIC EXPLANATIONS

Thanks to scientists, we are able to find out about the animals which came before mammals. Scientists study fossils, reconstruct skeletons and do their best to explain evolution and mass extinction.

Dinosaur extinction

Why did the dinosaurs disappear 65 million years ago? Researchers have come up with several explanations: ice ages, climate change, volcanoes, diseases... The most widely accepted theory is that a meteorite collided with Earth.
There is evidence that an object made of rock, metal or ice fell in Mexico and left a crater over 180km in diameter.

The meteorite fell in the Yucatán peninsula (Mexico).

A solid object with a diameter up to 10km collided with the planet Earth.

The shock wave travelled at 16km per second, instantly destroying everything in its path due to the intense heat that was generated. It caused enormous tidal waves and earthquakes.

The meteorite theory

The meteorite had immediate and long-term destructive consequences.

The heat generated by the impact (greater than the heat produced by millions of nuclear bombs) obliterated everything and caused devastating fires.

Dinosaurs and some other animal and plant species could not survive these effects, and they died.

It has been calculated that the impact of the meteorite caused strong earthquakes measuring 10 on the Richter scale, and huge seaquakes with enormous waves.

The heat and fires filled the atmosphere with ashes and dust particles which darkened the sky and caused the temperature of the Earth to drop.

115

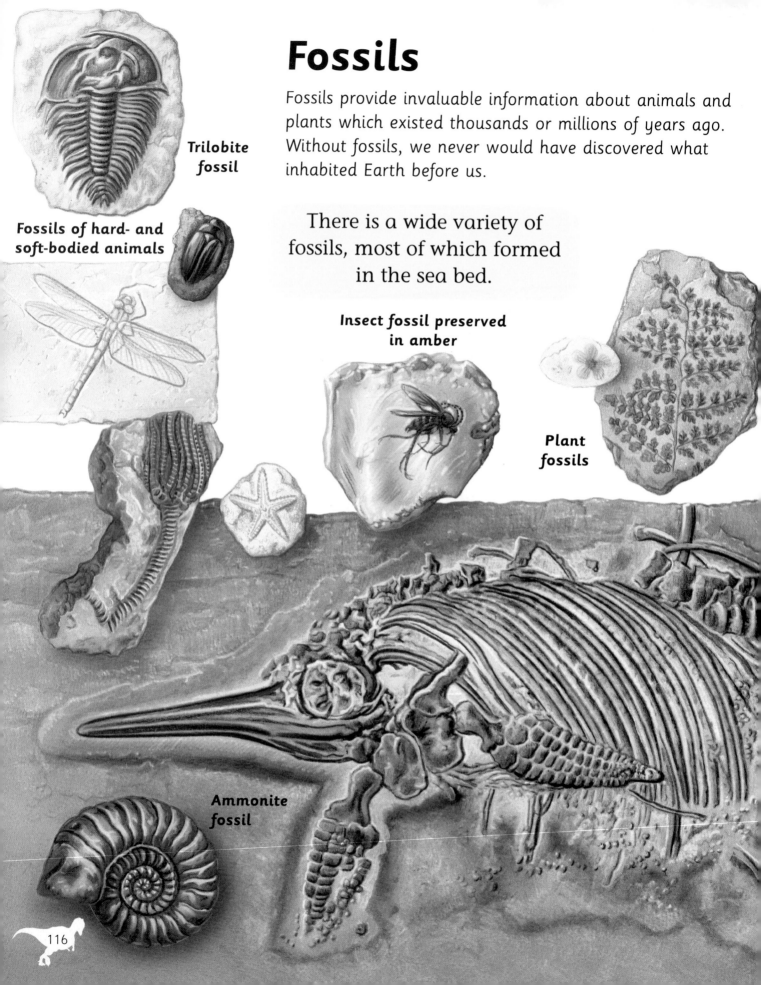

Fossils

Fossils provide invaluable information about animals and plants which existed thousands or millions of years ago. Without fossils, we never would have discovered what inhabited Earth before us.

There is a wide variety of fossils, most of which formed in the sea bed.

Trilobite fossil

Fossils of hard- and soft-bodied animals

Insect fossil preserved in amber

Plant fossils

Ammonite fossil

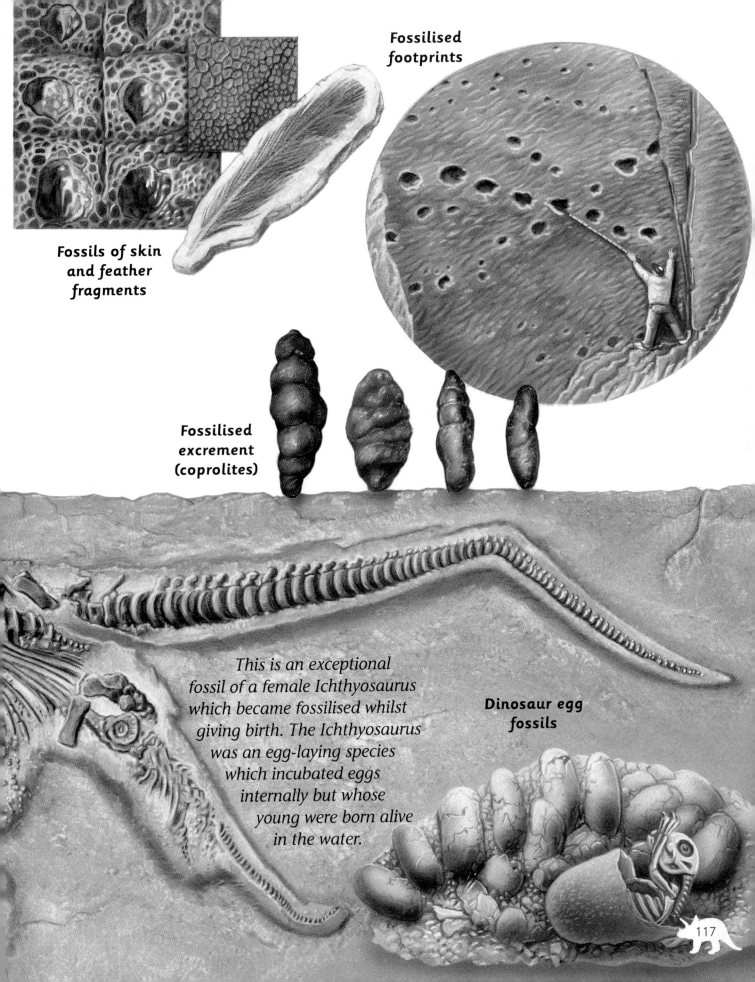

Fossils of skin
and feather
fragments

Fossilised
footprints

Fossilised
excrement
(coprolites)

This is an exceptional
fossil of a female Ichthyosaurus
which became fossilised whilst
giving birth. The Ichthyosaurus
was an egg-laying species
which incubated eggs
internally but whose
young were born alive
in the water.

Dinosaur egg
fossils

How fossils form

Step 1

Step 2

A fossil forms from the accumulation of sediment on the body before it decomposes. It takes place more easily in the sea, where the sedimentation of sand is continuous.

In general, only the hard parts of the body become fossilised, like bones, teeth and shell.

These steps show how a dead Tyrannosaurus becomes fossilised:

1. *The dead dinosaur is covered by the ocean or a river and is soon buried by mud.*

2. *Some years later, only the bones remain under new layers of sediment which keep building up.*

3. *Tens of millions of years later, the layers of sediment have moved and have become rock. The bones have gone, leaving a hollow mould which is then filled by minerals.*

4. *Over time, the sediment breaks and begins to erode.*

5. *The rock erodes to such an extent that the fossils begin to show on the surface, ready for palaeontologists to recover.*

Step 3

Step 4

Step 5

119

Dinosaurs in museums

Once the dinosaur is pieced back together, it may be put on show for everyone to see. Museums, films and books keep us interested in learning about these intriguing animals which lived on our planet many years before us.

It is fascinating to stand in front of a skeleton of Diplodocus or Tyrannosaurus rex. How impressive!

This Diplodocus is 26m long and would have weighed more than 10 tons.

Inside the dinosaur

Palaeontologists study fossilised bones in order to find the fixing points of the muscles. This is how they are able to work out their shape and reconstruct the entire body of a dinosaur.

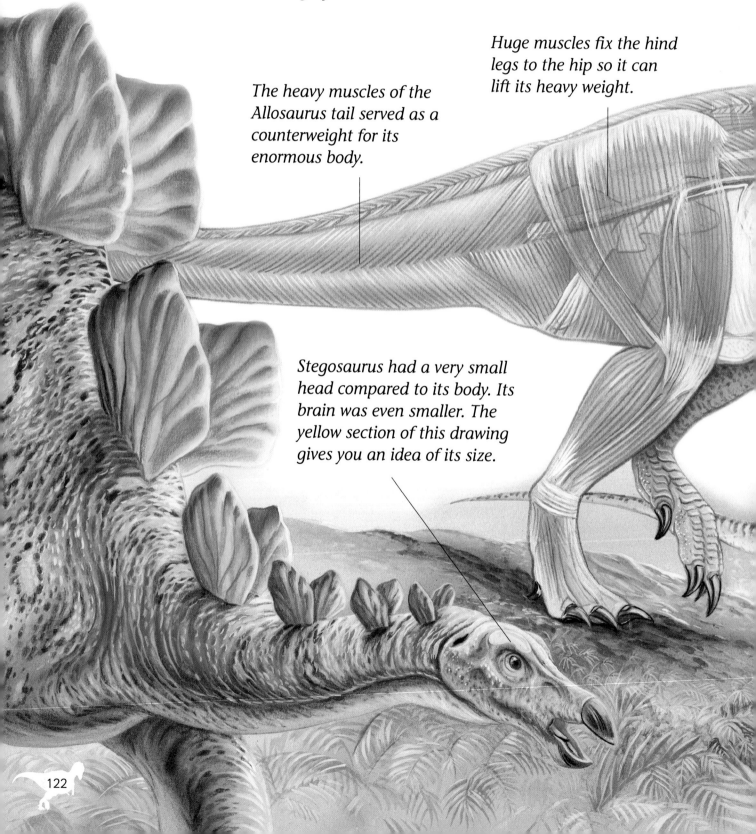

The heavy muscles of the Allosaurus tail served as a counterweight for its enormous body.

Huge muscles fix the hind legs to the hip so it can lift its heavy weight.

Stegosaurus had a very small head compared to its body. Its brain was even smaller. The yellow section of this drawing gives you an idea of its size.

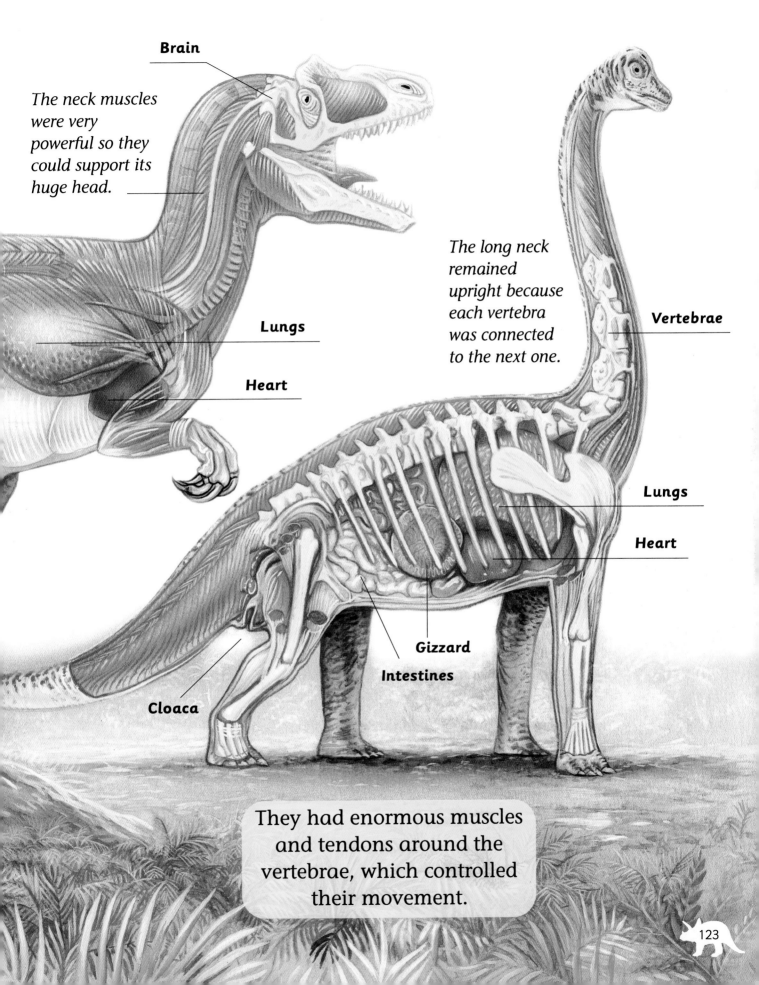

Brain

The neck muscles were very powerful so they could support its huge head.

The long neck remained upright because each vertebra was connected to the next one.

Vertebrae

Lungs

Heart

Lungs

Heart

Gizzard

Intestines

Cloaca

They had enormous muscles and tendons around the vertebrae, which controlled their movement.

Dinosaur Index

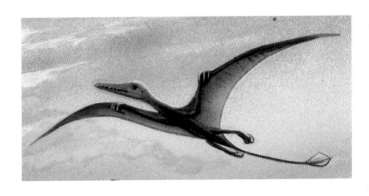